DEALER

M000306003

English Pewter Touchmarks

Including the marks of origin of
some of the Scottish and Irish Pewterers

by Radway Jackson

Edited and Introduced
by RONALD F. MICHAELIS

W. Foulsham & Co. Ltd
Yeovil Road, Slough, Berks, England
LONDON · NEW YORK · TORONTO · SYDNEY · CAPE TOWN

W. Foulsham & Co. Ltd,
Yeovil Road, Slough, Berks, England

ISBN 0-572-00743-4
Printed in Great Britain by
St Edmundsbury Press Ltd, Bury St Edmunds, Suffolk.

Contents

Acknowledgement

The Arms illustrated on the Cover are those borne on the Staff of the Beadle of the Worshipful Company of Pewterers at Pewterers Hall. The publishers extend their thanks to the Company for their permission to reproduce this piece and for their assistance in general.

Foreword

The compiler of this book has realised the need for a pocket-sized guide to pewter marks, and has produced an exceedingly worthwhile book. It will, I am sure, prove of inestimable benefit to those collectors of British pewterware who do not have access to more expensive, or more voluminous, literature on pewterers' touches, such as the late H. H. Cotterell's *Old Pewter, its Makers and Marks*, which is at present (and is likely to be for many years to come) the standard work, and the "Collectors' Bible".

Whilst it is a pleasurable thing to be able to find a legible touchmark on any piece of antique pewter, and to be able to refer to published literature to find out who was the maker; where his provenance, and what his period of working, it should not be thought that pewterware without any discernible mark is, necessarily, of any less merit. In some cases a mark has been lost through continual cleaning or scouring, and yet the piece itself is eminently 'collectable'; thus the student will need more than just a knowledge of makers and their marks in order to determine to what category such a piece belongs; for example, whether of good or poor metal; fine workmanship or design; English or foreign; antique or modern. The answers to these questions can come only from experience after handling and studying all specimens which may come to notice. It is in the course of these studies that the collector will have found many pieces with marks or touches which can be identified and dated, and from the styles of those he will, in the process of time, be able to allocate to nearly every piece at least a country of origin. Some specimens will be found with a mark, or marks, which are not recorded here nor, perhaps, even in larger and more comprehensive works; if so, it would be a wise precaution to record the mark by taking a clear rubbing with a lead pencil, or by making a drawing of *all that can be seen of it*. The collector should not attempt to draw in some part which is completely illegible, according to what he *thinks* it should be, or on the assumption that the missing part must have been symmetrical with that which is still discernible. In conjunction with the rubbed or drawn record he should make a note of the types of article upon which the marks were found, and their approximate dates, if known, for future reference. Who knows but that he may be able to pass on to posterity some useful data?

Most serious collectors will sooner or later make contact with other enthusiasts, perhaps by joining a society of collectors, and it is then that their knowledge can be passed on, and put to some real purpose.

Whereas the collectors of pewterware were ill-served in the earlier years of the present century by the lack of authoritative literature, there has been a very real attempt on the part of a few dedicated writers in the past few years to disseminate their knowledge in published form. During the last fifteen years there have appeared some seven or eight books and some dozens of useful magazine articles on antique pewterware, and details of many of these will be found in the attached bibliography. This spread of knowledge has enabled more and more collectors to appreciate the beauty and value of their finds, and thus pewter collecting today enjoys as much popularity as other acquisitive hobbies, such as silver, glass, porcelain, clocks or firearms collecting.

All the marks shown here have been well drawn from actual rubbings from the London touchplates, or from good photographs, and the handy size of the volume itself should appeal to those enthusiasts who may wish to carry it with them whilst on the hunt for the productions of the earlier British pewterers.

R.F.M.

Introduction

The object of this handbook is to put at the disposal of the searcher for antique pewterware a handy source of reference to enable him to determine the name of the maker, and the approximate date, of almost any piece of marked British pewterware which may come to his notice. The marks shown are the main "touchmarks", one of which *should* appear on all good class ware, but despite the fact that the Pewterers' Guilds – the Worshipful Company of Pewterers, in the case of London, and others in the provinces and in Scotland – decreed that all pewter should be marked by the maker, much of it, quite obviously, has never been so marked. In such cases, it does not necessarily follow, that the article is of inferior quality in metal or workmanship, but probably that the maker was too lax or too busy to strike his mark on every piece of a 'garnish'. There may be other reasons which will be indicated in the following pages. Often, too, the maker has used one of his secondary marks, for example a Rose and Crown mark, or his "hallmarks", instead of his main touch, and where these appear alone this may well make attribution more difficult.

This book would need to be of very much greater size and scope to encompass all the supplementary marks used by pewterers over the years, but if it were so comprehensive it would obviously defeat its object of being a "pocket guide". What is contained here is a reproduction of the touch of practically every London maker, from *c.* 1666 onwards, with a few others of from *c.* 1640. These, together with all the main touchmarks which appear on the Edinburgh touchplates, and some of the more prevalent marks found on English provincial and Irish wares, make a total of more than 1,200 drawings.

In the text which follows some information will be given on the regulations governing the striking of marks; the types of marks allowed to be used; the method of recording their ownership, and the allocation of new touchmarks by the Worshipful Company of Pewterers of London.

The touchmark of George Grenfell, London, inside the base of a George II domed-lid tankard, c. 1750-60 (with enlargement, inset)

It would be a very desirable situation if every piece of pewterware which the collector is able to pick up were to bear a recognisable touchmark, and even more so if he were then able to refer to the tables of marks in this volume and find out something about it. Unfortunately, this is not always possible, nor is it likely that any one volume could aspire to that completeness. It also happens that some of the choicest specimens are found to be entirely devoid of any sign of an original touchmark, while others have only traces of a mark once clearly defined but now so worn away as to be almost unrecognisable. Even of those with clear touchmarks perhaps only some will be found herein; of the others it is also possible that a number may not be traced even in any other available literature. The reason may be (i) that the earlier compilers have not previously come across that particular mark or maker, (ii) that the mark was not found sufficiently well defined to copy or, (iii) that the markings are of continental origin.

No one volume could possibly incorporate all the known marks of all provenances, nor, indeed, could any one compiler accept the mammoth task of bringing them together from all corners of the globe where pewter-making has taken place. Take, for instance, the marks on German pewterware alone: one author has already produced a series of seven volumes of such information (the last published in 1937), and it is by no means exhaustive. Many other writers have attempted the task with reference to the pewterware of their own particular country, and so the volume of accumulated material is now so great that one can hope to tackle the study only by stages. Collectors in Britain tend to specialise in the pieces produced within the British Isles, and it is for them that this smaller work has been produced.

The main touchmark of a London pewterer,
Robert Lucas, c. 1640, with his "hallmarks".

THE EARLY HISTORY OF PEWTER MARKS

As early as the year 1503 the marking of pewterware was made compulsory by directives of the guilds governing the trade, and, in 1550 in London, the Pewterers' Company

Two dishes with multiple-reeded rims, bearing "hallmarks"
at front, of John Raymond, London, c. 1690-95

records mention an inventory which contains the item "a table of pewter with every man's mark thereon". Again, in 1592, it was ordered that "all the Company shall set their touches on a new plate". Although the first mention of a "table" (or touchplate) appears at the middle of the sixteenth century such records must have existed for many decades prior to this, but, whether recorded in the Hall or not, there is ample evidence that London pewterers were allowed the use of touches personal to themselves. In 1487 reference is made to one Walter Walsh and his wife Katherine who presented spoons to the Company "with his mark and name on one, and on the other Saint Katherine". In 1492 we read that the Company bought "a new marking iron for hollow-ware men". (This would most probably have been the punch to mark the pewter lids of pottery vessels, for which the Beadle of the Company received a fee for "vewing and markyng".) In 1548 another marking iron was purchased; this time its device is stated to be the fleur-de-lis, and its purpose "to amarked stone pots with". ("Stone pots" were, of course, pottery, or stoneware, vessels to which pewter lids were affixed by the pewterers). In 1552 an order required all stone pots to be marked on the inside of the lid with the maker's mark, and on the outside with "the mark of the Hall" (i.e. the above-mentioned fleur-de-lis). This order was rescinded in 1558, insofar as "the mark of the Hall" was concerned, but makers were still to place their own marks inside the lids. Other marks of particular significance were (in 1474) the "puncheon of iron with broad arrow, for the forfeit mark", and (1509) a "marking iron of the Strake of Tin and Lilypot"; there is no doubt as to the purpose of the former, although it is doubtful if any pieces marked with the "punch of the broad arrow" still remain – they would have been destroyed after the maker had been duly punished for the production of inferior ware. With regard to the mark of 1509 there is no evidence to indicate its significance, but one may hazard a guess that it was a mark of quality or appraisal, for both the strake and the lilypot are devices drawn in the margin of the Grant of Arms to the Company in 1533, and the strake itself was repeated thrice in the heraldic shield.

The Tudor Rose, which is also included in the Arms (and repeated in the margin of this important parchment) was itself later adopted as a mark of quality. In 1572 new ordinances confirmed several older edicts relating to the marking of pewterware, and it was agreed then that "every one of the fellowship that maketh any ware shall set his own mark thereon, and that no man shall give for his proper mark or touch the Rose and Crown with letters or otherwise, but only him to whom it was given by the fellowship". At a later date (1672) it was decreed "that from henceforth no person or persons whatsoever shall presume to strike the rose and crown with any additional flourish, or the letters of his own or another's name, whereby [? lest] the mark which is only to be used for goods exported may, in time, become as other touches and not distinguished". It should be noted that the Rose and Crown marks used by London makers could formerly have been struck in conjunction with the maker's name in full, or with his initials only; in the latter cases they would have been placed one at each side of the mark, *never* in the crown itself, which was a continental practice.

Finally "no man of the craft shall give another's mark, neither with letters or otherwise, but everyone to give a sundry mark, such one as shall be allowed by the Master and Wardens for the time being". It will be seen that very close control was maintained over all marks, whether personal or official, from the earliest times and it is regrettable that no tangible records remain of the touches of individual pewterers prior to the time of the Great Fire in 1666. In that year the earlier touchplates and many other records were lost. In 1667 some attempt was made to collect together the marks of existing London pewterers who had survived, and a new touchplate which was then brought into being contains several marks of earlier date. In addition to these re-struck marks all newly-made freemen were required to record the touches granted to them when they were permitted to "open shop". This permission was given only when the Court of the Pewterers' Company was satisfied that the newly-fledged pewterer was a capable craftsman, and had sufficient capital for the purpose.

To attain the proper status, an apprentice, upon being made "free" (after having been bound for, perhaps, seven or ten years) might continue to work for his former tutor, or become a journeyman for an established master, for several more years.

The five London touchplates contain records of marks in the

order in which they were granted (on the first plate only are these interspersed with a few earlier touches) and so, from 1667 to c. 1820, there was maintained a virtually complete record of London makers' touches. There are, nevertheless, marks of many other working pewterers, known to have been apprenticed in London but who returned to their home area or to work in the provinces, whose marks do not appear. From time to time a touch on a piece of pewterware made outside London can be attributed to one of these men by virtue of the device and initials in it. It frequently happened that a young pewterer (with permission) adopted the motifs of, or devices similar to those which had been used by, his former master or his own relatives, and it is when these can be linked to him by the inclusion of his own initials, or name in full, that one can be reasonably sure of the correctness of the attribution.

There can be little doubt that records of touches, on touchplates similar to those of London, were maintained by the guilds in most of the large pewtering centres (certainly at York, and probably in many Scottish towns) but only in one instance, that of Edinburgh, have they come to light.

At Edinburgh, two touchplates (the first with marks from c. 1590 to c. 1760, and the other with two later marks only) were found in 1871, in somewhat curious circumstances. In that year an ancient chest containing the two touchplates and some other objects was presented to the National Museum of Antiquities of that city; the box had been in the possession of the famous "Johnny Faa", and it was then assumed that the marks on the touchplates were "licences" to the tribe of gypsies, of which Johnny Faa and his descendants were the leaders, to work at the hammermen's crafts. In due course, however, the true significance of the marks was discovered. They were, in fact, the recorded touchmarks of pewterers belonging to the Edinburgh Incorporation of Hammermen, and it was presumed that, as the touches ended abruptly in 1764 (with only two marks struck on the second plate), the records had probably been stolen about then by a member of the gypsy clan, and had remained hidden ever since.

There is, of course, still the remotest chance that the touchplates of some other pewterers' guilds are extant, tucked away in some remote corner of an attic or cellar, but until they are unearthed there is little hope of being able to allocate many hundreds of known marks to their original owners. In some cases only a guess can be made as to their locality. There are some clues to be obtained from the devices used in these marks; for example, it was not an uncommon practice for Bristol makers to use the Fleur-de-lis as the central feature of the touch; for York pewterers to use the Lamb and Flag; for some Scottish makers the Edinburgh Castle mark, and some Irish makers the Harp.

"Hallmarks" used by Robert Clothyer, of Chard, Somerset, on a dish of c. 1695

SUPPLEMENTARY MARKS

"Hall-marks"

Supplementary marks, usually four in number, grouped together like silver hall-marks, may sometimes also help to indicate the provenance of the maker. Scottish pewterers frequently used a Thistle as one of these small "hall-marks", and Irish makers often adopted the figure of Hibernia, or a Harp; Bristol pewterers, again, used either a Fleur-de-lis, a Griffin's head, or a figure of Britannia in one or more of the small shields.

"Hall-marks" on pewter, so called for their likeness to those on silver, differ from them in this respect; they have no function in deciding the date of manufacture or the maker. They were added, undoubtedly, to attempt to simulate silverware; indeed newly wrought and polished pewter could, and did, look extremely like it, and the additional marks could deceive the onlooker who viewed the pieces on a dresser some yards away!

The main touchmark of a Bristol partnership,
and their "hallmarks".

The earliest mention in the London Pewterers' Company records of "marks proper to the Goldsmiths" is in 1635, at which time the Goldsmiths' Company complained of "a certain plate, made of pewter, having the stamps and marks upon it which only belongeth to the Companie of Goldsmiths of London, as if it had been of silver plate of the assaye of the said Companie".

It seems that little notice was taken of the order to discontinue the practice, for it is the exception rather than the rule for any seventeenth-century plate or dish to be found without simulated hall-marks. In 1681 one John Blackwell was admonished "for selling plates without any other mark than the silver mark", and as late as 1754 the brothers Cleeve were allowed to dispose of twelve dozen plates "bearing only their silver marks". Such secondary marks dropped out of general use somewhere about this time, although a few makers continued to use marks of similar character even into the earlier years of the next century.

It was the more common practice for one or more of the "hall-marks" to contain the initials which appeared in the main touch, but instances occur where the "hall-marks" appear with another man's initials or devices, and in such cases one may assume that the piece was made by the maker who struck the *touch*, for this was compulsory, whereas the smaller marks were not – indeed, at times they were expressly forbidden!

Where differences do occur, the explanation is almost certain to be that the piece was made (i) for resale by another pewterer or factor, who desired some advertisement of his own to appear on it, (ii) by a partnership of two established pewterers, or (iii) by a pewterer succeeding to the business of another; examples of all these categories will be found.

"Labels"

At times the use of advertising "labels" was prohibited, and at others allowed in some restricted form. In the first instance some pewterers were granted permission to include the word "LONDON" in their marks; at a later date some used an additional label bearing this word alone.

A label may say, merely, "Made in London", "London Superfine", "Superfine French Metal" or "English Block Tin" (the latter label being sometimes used in Ireland). These marks, although not touches in any true sense of the word, vary in detail, since they were struck from individually engraved dies, and thus may frequently be found to be of assistance in deciding the country or town of origin (and sometimes even the maker). Nevertheless, they should not always be taken too literally; several provincial pewterers have used, without authority, a label similar to that of a London maker. One in particular, John Duncomb, a Birmingham maker, who had been specifically excluded from the London Company in 1706, used a label bearing only the word "LONDON", and went even further in including in another mark (used in conjunction with it) the words: "John Duncomb, Freeman of". The word "LONDON" has, too, been used on continental and American ware, to denote that it was *made of tin from London*.

"X" Crowned

The "X" with crown above is frequently found, either alone, or in conjunction with a main touch. Originally this was intended as a quality mark, as the following extract from the

Pewterers' Company records will show: "1690–91. Complaint was made against Samuel Hancock for striking his name at length upon his trencher plates, and at each end thereof is struck his own touch and the Rose and Crown, and for striking the letter X upon ordinary ware, which is a mark generally used by the Mistery to distinguish extraordinary ware".

In the course of time however, as was the case with most other of the Company's edicts, this restriction came to be ignored, and the mark has been used haphazardly, particularly on quite late tavern pots and measures, some of which can lay no honest claim to high quality.

Capacity, or Verification, "Seals"

Marks of various kinds, quite distinct from makers' marks, and having no relationship whatsoever to them, may be found on the rims, or occasionally on the lids, of pots and measures which have been in use in places where liquids were sold to the public.

(a)   (b)   (c)

From very ancient times standards of measure have been in force for wines, ale and other liquids, and inspectors were appointed to check that the vessels in which they were retailed did, in fact, contain the correct quantity. If a measure did not hold a volume in accordance with the standard then in force, it was confiscated and destroyed; if it was found to be of true capacity, then a mark, or "seal" was struck on it to verify this fact. It should be remembered that the standards themselves have varied from time to time, but in the reign of Henry VII considerable progress was made in bringing some uniformity out of the chaos which had existed formerly; in 1497 the "Winchester gallon", of 268.43 cubic inches capacity

(155.16 fluid ozs.), for "Wheate, Wyne and Ale" was introduced. Other monarchs sanctioned variations of the Winchester gallon; that of Elizabeth I, of 1601, was so close that little attention appears to have been paid to it, although some localities interpreted the standard incorrectly, and a measure of 282 cu. ins. (163.00 fl. ozs.) was adopted. This became a "Customary" measure, which was later legalised by William III, in 1688, when separate standards for wine and ale were introduced. The Ale gallon was retained at 282 cu. ins., and a Wine gallon at 224 cu. ins. was adopted. The Ale gallon was amended very slightly in 1702.

(d)   (e)

It is necessary to have some appreciation of the foregoing facts to understand the meaning of some of the earlier "seals" which may, otherwise, puzzle the finder. A measure, for instance, bearing on the neck a mark similar in character to (a), (b) or (c) above, was "sealed" by an inspector because it conformed to the standard of Henry VII. Several measures, of dates prior to c. 1600 have been found with Crowned "hR" marks, and others, which may have been made some 50 or 100 years later, also have been "sealed" with somewhat similar marks, although sometimes the first initial is a capital "H".

"Seals" of "W.R" Crowned (d) above, are found on measures dating from c. 1688 onwards, and may still be found on vessels made as late as the end of the eighteenth century. The reason is that the William III "Customary" Ale gallon was found to be that to which the pot in question conformed, i.e. it was the legal standard accepted by the inspector detailed to check its capacity.

In 1704, and again in 1707, Queen Anne introduced variations to former standards, but only the Wine gallon, then of 231

cu. ins. (133.54 fl. ozs.), seems to have gained popular acceptance, and became the standard adopted for this commodity
for the remainder of the century and, indeed, until 1824 when
all former standards were made illegal in favour of the newly
introduced Imperial measure. Thus, occasionally, one may
find a capacity seal corresponding to (e) above.

In 1824 all former standards were abandoned, and only if a
pot was found to contain not less than an Imperial quart or
pint, as the case might be, was it "sealed" with a verification
mark; this was frequently of the type shown at (e). Other
forms of verification seal were used in different localities; some
being merely initial letters denoting the town or county
district, for example YNR (Yorkshire, North Riding) and
CO-ED (County of Edinburgh), others being the town crest
or emblem. The variations are far too numerous to list here.

(f)

In 1878 the Board of Trade introduced a stamp of uniform
design for all localities, comprising the sovereign's initials,
crowned, and with numerals below (as (f) above): the number
indicating the town or county authority to which that number
had been exclusively allotted; thus, with a knowledge of the
districts to which these seals were given, one can define the
area of usage of the measure concerned. Although the latter
types of seal were introduced only in 1878 it does not follow
that all measures bearing such marks are of that late date.
Obviously, if a measure had been made any time after 1824
(and thus to Imperial scale) *and was still in use in 1878 or later*,
it would be so marked; similarly some measures of pre-1824
manufacture *which conformed closely* to the newly-adopted
Imperial standard (*and were not less* in capacity) might bear
later "seals" denoting their acceptance.

It will be seen, therefore, that a capacity seal of 1878 type
need not, in every case, decide the period of manufacture of

(g)   (h)   (i)

the vessel on which it appears; the measure could have been made earlier than 1878 but not "sealed" until then, or after.

The now commonly accepted crowned initial and numeral seal was adapted for Edward VII and later sovereigns by variation of the initials, as in (g) and (h).

Some areas are known to have applied actual year stampings in addition to the compulsory official seal, and one may find measures with a succession of numeral stampings "78", "86", "94" and so on (denoting that they were examined in the years 1878, 1886 or 1894, etc., as the case may be).

One further stamping needs mention, and it is the "G.R." which appears struck on the neck of some Channel Islands measures. This may be taken to indicate George V, during whose reign, in 1915, the Imperial standard was eventually adopted, to the exclusion of the various other standards formerly in use in those islands. It seems that measures, of whatever date made, but found then to conform closely to Imperial scale, were "sealed" with this mark. It is somewhat confusing, however, to find it also on some other Channel Islands measures, made to either the local standard, or to metric measure, and one wonders just what reliance can be placed on it. Space here does not allow one to conjecture, but this is a possible field of study for the future.

Marks of Ownership
Finally, mention must be made of the plain initials which have been struck with individual punches, sometimes on the back, and sometimes on the front of the rim of plates and dishes, set in a form similar to one or another of the following examples:

A T W B G F W M
          (crowned) (crowned) D

In every case these will be merely the initials of a former owner
– not necessarily the original possessor, for sometimes more
than one set of initials may be found – and are unlikely to be of
any help in deciding a date or the locality of an object unless, of
course, there is any other corroboratory evidence as to the
names of the respective owners.

Crowned ownership initials are shown in the illustration
below.

*English Porringer, c. 1700, showing crowned ownership
initials*

There is nothing to indicate that initials with a crown above
had, necessarily, any royal or other significance, and it must be
assumed that, where so used, it was merely a form of snobbery,
or perhaps because the pewterer who struck them at the
owner's request had no other available punches. In the cases of
initials set in triangular formation, these may be taken to
represent the surname, at top, and the Christian names of both

husband and wife below; for example, Davison, William and Margaret would conveniently fit the example shown above.

Left *English baluster-shaped Wine Measure, showing the owner's "housemarks", and his initials on the handle*

Right *A galaxy of owners' indicated by fifteen sets of initials on the lid of a tavern measure, of c. 1740*

This is of an English baluster-shaped Wine Measure, upon which the pewterer's touchmark is struck on the neck, at right of the handle (although it cannot be clearly seen in the photograph). On the lid has been struck repeatedly a punch bearing the words "EDWd. SEYMOUR · FLEET STR." around the device of a posthorn within a circle.

The individually punched letters "E" and "S" also appear at the top of the handle. It is known that, in this case, its erstwhile owner, one Edward Seymour, was the tenant of the tavern "Ye Horn in ye Hoop" in Fleet Street, London, from c. 1720 to 1734. The punches upon the lid are known to collectors as "housemarks", and when attributable to known individuals or taverns, can add considerable interest to an otherwise prosaic piece.

Touchmarks

GEORGE
ABBOTT
—
LONDON
1664 – 1675

WILLIAM
ADAMS
—
LONDON
1646 – 1681

JAMES
ABERNETHIE
—
EDINBURGH
1640 –

THOMAS
ALDER
—
LONDON
1657 – 1680

JAMES
ABERNETHIE
—
EDINBURGH
1660 –

GEORGE
ALDERSON
—
LONDON
1728 – 1761

JAMES
ABERNETHIE
—
EDINBURGH
1669 –

SIR GEORGE
ALDERSON
—
LONDON
1817 – 1826

WILLIAM
ABERNETHIE
—
EDINBURGH
1649 –

JOHN
ALDERSON
—
LONDON
1766 – 1792

HENRY
ADAMS
—
LONDON
1685 – 1732

THOMAS
ALDERSON
—
LONDON
1790 – 1805

WILLIAM
ADAMS
—
LONDON
1676 – 1687

RICHARD
ALDERWICK
—
LONDON
1752 – 1771

RICHARD
ALDERWICK
—
LONDON
1776–

ROBERT
ALGER
—
LONDON
c. 1668

JOHN
ALLEN
—
LONDON
1671 – 1710

RICHARD
ALLEN
—
LONDON
1647 – 1675

WILLIAM
ALLEN
—
LONDON
1675 – 1686

BENNETT
(BENEDICT?)
ALLETT
—
LONDON
1664 – 1675

ADAM
ANDERSON
—
EDINBURGH
1734–

WILLIAM
ANDERSON
—
EDINBURGH
1654–

JOHN
ANDERSONE
—
EDINBURGH
1693–

ROBERT
ANDERSONE
—
EDINBURGH
1697–

PHILEMON
ANGEL
—
LONDON
1684 – 1701

WILLIAM
GLOVER
ANNISON
—
LONDON
1746 – 1759

JOHN
ANSELL
—
LONDON
1717 – 1729

HENRY
APPLETON
—
LONDON
1750 – 1771

JOHN
APPLETON
—
LONDON
1775 – 1792

WILLIAM
ATTWOOD
—
LONDON
1683 – 1695

THOMAS
ARNOTT
—
LONDON
1706 –

JOSEPH
AUSTEN
—
CORK
c. 1815 – d. 1845

JAMES
ASHLEY
—
LONDON
1820 – 1851

WILLIAM
AYRES
—
LONDON
1663

THOMAS J. T.
ASHLEY
—
LONDON
1821 – 1852

BERNARD
BABB
—
LONDON
1700

WILLIAM
ATKINSON
—
LONDON
1672 – 1676

RICHARD
BACHE
—
LONDON
1783 – 1805

WILLIAM
ATLEE
—
LONDON
1696 –

BENJAMIN
BACON
—
LONDON
1759

ROBERT
ATTERTON
—
LONDON
1693 –

GEORGE
BACON
—
LONDON
1746 – 1771

THOMAS
BACON
—
LONDON
1724 – 1746

THOMAS
BARFORD
—
LONDON
1667 - 1675

RICHARD
BAGSHAW
—
LONDON
1786 – 1814

JOHN
BARLOW
—
LONDON
1699

WILLIAM
BALLANTYNE
—
EDINBURGH
1742 – d. 1748

THOMAS
BARNES
—
LONDON
1728 – 1741

WILLIAM
BALLANTYNE
—
EDINBURGH
1749 – 1775

WILLIAM
BARNES
—
LONDON
1776

WILLIAM
BAMPTON
—
LONDON
1749 – 1799

ROBERT
BARNETT
—
LONDON
1788 – 1829

NATHANIEL
BARBER
—
LONDON
1777 – 1788

DANIEL
BARTON
—
LONDON
1670 – 1699

RICHARD
BARFORD
—
LONDON
1674

DANIEL
BARTON
—
LONDON
1678

DANIEL BARTON — LONDON 1700		GEORGE BEESTON — LONDON 1749 – 1768	
JOHN BASKERVILLE — LONDON 1691 – 1702		RICHARD BELSHER — LONDON 1674 – 1680	
JOHN BATCHELER — BRISTOL c. 1680 – 1727		JOHN BELSON — LONDON 1738 – 1783	
WILLIAM BATHUS — LONDON 1798 – 1805		BENNETT & CHAPMAN — LONDON 1761	
THOMAS BATTESON — LONDON 1666 – 1668		THOMAS BENNETT — LONDON 1700	
WILLIAM BEAMONT — LONDON 1711		THOMAS BENNET — BRISTOL c. 1760 – 1780	
THOMAS BECKETT — LONDON 1703 – 1731		WILLIAM BENNETT — LONDON 1762	

JOHN
BENSON
—
LONDON
1740 – 1752

JOHN
BLENMAN
—
LONDON
1726 – d. 1727

RALPH
BENTON
—
LONDON
1676 – 1693

JOHN
BLEWETT
—
LONDON
1708

NATHANIEL
BESSANT
—
LONDON
1702

JOHN
BLUNT
—
LONDON
1679 – 1681

THOMAS
BETTS
—
LONDON
1680 – 1686

THOMAS
BOARDMAN
—
LONDON
1741 – 1773

JAMES
BISHOP
—
LONDON
1724

JONATHAN
BONKIN
—
LONDON
1678

BENJAMIN
BLACKWELL
—
LONDON
1678 – 1712

JONATHAN
BONKIN
—
LONDON
1717

JOHN
BLAKE
—
LONDON
not known

BON [ENGLISH PEWTER TOUCHMARKS]

ENGLISH PEWTER TOUCHMARKS

JOHN BONVILLE — LONDON 1682 – 1686	BEZA BOSTON — LONDON 1664 – 1685
JAMES BOOST — LONDON 1751 – 1774	JABEZ BOSTON — LONDON 1671 – 1686
ROBERT BOR(D)MAN (BOARDMAN) — LONDON 1701 – 1738	THOMAS BOSWORTH — LONDON 1699
THOMAS BOULTON — WIGAN c. 1760 – 1798	JOHN BOTELER — LONDON 1743 – 1755
ANDRO BORTHWICK — EDINBURGH 1620	RICHARD BOWCHER — LONDON 1727
WILLIAM BORTHWICK — EDINBURGH 1653 – d. 1654	JOSEPH BOWDEN — LONDON 1697 – 1721
SAMUEL BOSS — LONDON 1701 – 1718	HENRY BOWLER — LONDON 1757 – 1779

32

RICHARD BOWLER — LONDON 1762	RICHARD BRA(D)FIELD — LONDON 1685
SAMUEL SALTER BOWLER — LONDON 1779	PETER BRAILESFORD — LONDON 1661 – 1678
BENJAMIN BOYDEN — LONDON 1694 – 1700	WILLIAM BRAINE — LONDON 1681
THOMAS BOYDEN — LONDON 1707	HENRY BRASTED — LONDON 1696
HENRY BRADLEY — LONDON 1676 – 1678	WILLIAM BRAVELL — LONDON 1692 – 1702
EDWARD BRADSTREET — LONDON 1726	HENRY BRETTELL — LONDON c. 1657
RICHARD BRADSTREET — LONDON 1730	JAMES BRETTELL — LONDON 1690 – 1692

STEPHEN
BRIDGES
—
LONDON
1696 – 1719

DAVID
BROOKS
—
LONDON
1702

JOHN
BRODHURST
—
LONDON
1720 – 1738

JOHN
BROMFIELD
—
LONDON
1745

JOSEPH
BROOKER
—
LONDON
1682

ALEXANDER
BROWN
—
EDINBURGH
1702 – 1717

JOHN C.
BROWN
—
LONDON
1786 – 1836

JOHN & JOSEPH BROWN
and
JOHN LEWIS
—
LONDON 1764

RALPH
BROWN
—
LONDON
1669 – 1681

RICHARD
BROWN
—
LONDON
1730

WILLIAM
BROWN
—
LONDON
1705
(touch dated '75
in error)

BENJAMIN
BROWNE
—
LONDON
1727 – 1738

JOHN
BROWNE
—
EDINBURGH
1761 – 1773

MARTIN
BROWNE
—
LONDON
1695 – 1703

THOMAS
BUCKBY
—
LONDON
1701 – 1732

ROBERT
BROWNE
—
EDINBURGH
1733 – 1745

WILLIAM
BUCKLEY
—
LONDON
1690

WILLIAM
BROWNE
—
EDINBURGH
1729 – d. 1741

JAMES
BUCLENNAND
—
EDINBURGH
1643

BROWNE &
SWANSON
—
LONDON
1760

DAVID
BUDDEN , Sr.
—
LONDON
1669

EGERTON
BRYAN
—
LONDON
1674 – 1681

DAVID
BUDDEN , Jr.
—
LONDON
1702

DAVID
BRYCE
—
EDINBURGH
1654

JOHN
BULL
—
LONDON
1661 – 1693

ALEXANDER
BRYDEN
—
EDINBURGH
1704

JAMES
BULLEVANT
—
LONDON
1661 – 1680

JAMES
BULLOCK
—
LONDON
1750 – 1754

WILLIAM
BURTON
—
LONDON
1660 – 1683

EDWARD
BUNKELL
—
EDINBURGH
1728 – d. 1756

WILLIAM
BURTON
—
LONDON
1660 – 1683

EDWARD
BURCHALL
—
LONDON
1682 – 1690

ROBERT
BUSH
—
BRISTOL
c. 1755 – 1785

BURFORD &
GREEN
—
LONDON
1748 – 1780

ROBERT
BUSH & CO.
—
BRISTOL
c. 1790 – 1793

THOMAS
BURGES
—
LONDON
1701

THOMAS
BUTTERY
—
LONDON
1692 – 1721

ROBERT
BURNS
—
EDINBURGH
1694

THOMAS
BUTTERY
—
LONDON
1757

MUNGO
BURTON
—
EDINBURGH
1709

WILLIAM
BUTTERY
—
LONDON
1686

JOHN
BUXTON
—
LONDON
1668

JOSEPH
CABLE
—
LONDON
1682 – d. 1707

JOHN
CALCOTT
—
LONDON
1701

JOHN
CAMBRIDGE
—
LONDON
1687

GEORGE
CANBY
—
LONDON
1695

JOHN
CARPENTER
—
LONDON
1701

JOHN
CARPENTER
—
LONDON
1717 – d. 1747

CARPENTER &
HAMBERGER
—
LONDON
1794 – 1805

JOHN
CARR
—
LONDON
1696

JOHN
CARR
—
LONDON
1723 – 1737

JAMES
CARTER
—
LONDON
1683 – 1704

JOSEPH
CARTER
—
LONDON
1726

PETER
CARTER
—
LONDON
1699 – 1704

THOMAS
CARTWRIGHT
—
LONDON
1715 – 1750

THOMAS
CARY
—
LONDON
1686

THOMAS
CHAMBERLAIN
—
LONDON
1734

BENJAMIN
CASIMER
—
LONDON
1704 – 1722

RICHARD
CHAMBERS
—
YORK
1698 – 1738

JOHN
CASTLE
—
LONDON
1677 – 1686

CATESBY
CHAPMAN
—
LONDON
1721

THOMAS
CASTLE
—
LONDON
1689 – 1698

WILLIAM
CHARSLEY
—
LONDON
1732 – 1770

JOHN
CATER
—
LONDON
1725 – 1729

JOHN
CHILD
—
LONDON
1701

JOHN CAVE
(Senior & Junior)
—
BRISTOL
c. 1650/60 – 1710

LAWRENCE
CHILD
—
LONDON
1695 – 1727

THOMAS
CAVE
—
BRISTOL
c. 1684 – 1734

GEORGE
CHRICHTOUNE
—
EDINBURGH
1664

WILLIAM CHRISTIE — **EDINBURGH** 1652 – 1665		**RICHARD CLARK** — **LONDON** 1696	
CHARLES CLARIDGE — **LONDON** 1758 – 1817		**THOMAS CLARK** — **LONDON** 1680 – 1711	
JOSEPH CLARIDGE — **LONDON** 1727 – 1756		**WILLIAM CLARK** — **LONDON** 1691	
THOMAS CLARIDGE — **LONDON** 1717 – 1756		**WILLIAM CLARK** — **LONDON** 1696 – 1711	
CHRISTOPHER CLARK — **LONDON** 1672 – 1686		**WILLIAM CLARK** — **LONDON** 1721 – 1756	
JOSIAH CLARK — **LONDON** 1694		**CLARK & GREENING** — **LONDON** 1765	

JAMES
CLARKE
—
LONDON
1722

SAMUEL
COCKS
—
LONDON
1819

ALEXANDER
CLEEVE Sr.
—
LONDON
1689 – 1729

JOHN
COKE
—
LONDON
1694

ALEXANDER
CLEEVE Jr.
—
LONDON
1729 – 1748

JEREMIAH
COLE
—
LONDON
1679 – 1698

BOU(R)CHIER
CLEEVE
—
LONDON
1738

JOHN
COLE
—
LONDON
1727

GILES
CLEEVE
—
LONDON
1729 – d. 1743

THOMAS
COLLETT
—
LONDON
1735

FRANCIS
CLIFFE
—
LONDON
1690

JOSEPH
COLLIER
—
LONDON
1670 – 1712

THOMAS
COCKBURN
—
EDINBURGH
1711

PETER
COLLIER
—
LONDON
1720–1725

| RICHARD COLLIER — LONDON 1668 – 1679 | |
| WILLIAM COOCH — LONDON 1733 – 1756 | |

RICHARD COLLIER
—
LONDON
1707 – 1746

WILLIAM COOCH
—
LONDON
1775 – c. 1800

WILLIAM COLMAN
—
LONDON
1694

ISAAC COOKE
—
LONDON
1692 – 1700

JOSEPH COLSON
—
LONDON
1670 – 1686

SAMUEL COOKE
—
LONDON
1728 – 1732

JOHN COMPERE
—
LONDON
1699 – 1709

THOMAS COOKE
—
LONDON
1699 – 1718

THOMAS and TOWNSEND COMPTON
—
LONDON
1801 – 1817

WILLIAM COOKE
—
BRISTOL
1795 – 1812

COOKE & FREEMAN — LONDON 1732		GILBERT CORNHILL — LONDON 1670	
BENJAMIN COOPER — LONDON 1680 – 1727		BENJAMIN COTTON — LONDON 1682	
JOHN COOPER — LONDON 1682 – 1693		JONATHAN COTTON Sr. — LONDON 1705 – 1742	
JOHN COOPER — LONDON 1690		JONATHAN COTTON Jr. — LONDON 1736 – 1754	
THOMAS COOPER — LONDON 1654 – 1678		ALEXANDER COULTHARD — LONDON 1708	
THOMAS COOPER — LONDON 1679		JOHN COURSEY Sr. — LONDON 1663 – 1681	
JOHN CORMELL — LONDON 1684 – c. 1690		JOHN COURSEY Jr. — LONDON 1686	

THOMAS COWDEROY — LONDON 1691	
JOHN COWLEY — LONDON 1728 – 1742	
WILLIAM COWLEY — LONDON 1663 – 1710	
WILLIAM COWLING — LONDON 1740	
JAMES COWPER — EDINBURGH 1704	
JOHN COX — LONDON 1676 – 1685	
RICHARD COX — LONDON 1723	

WILLIAM COX — LONDON 1710	
CHARLES CRANLEY — LONDON 1694	
MARK CRIPPS — LONDON 1727 – 1776	
ROBERT CROOK — LONDON 1742	
WILLIAM CROOKE — LONDON 1681 – 1686	
JOHN CROPP — LONDON 1678 – 1687	
WILLIAM CROPP — LONDON 1659 – 1670	
ABRAHAM CROSS — LONDON 1716	

ROBERT CROSFIELD — LONDON 1707		RICHARD DALE — LONDON 1710	
JAMES CURTIS — BRISTOL c. 1770 – 1793		DARLING & MEAKIN — LONDON 1732 – 1760	
JOHN CUTHBERTSON — EDINBURGH 1712		JOHN DAVIS — LONDON 1722 – 1762	
THOMAS CUTLOVE — LONDON 1676 – d. 1680		WILLIAM DAVISONE — EDINBURGH 1691	
JOHN DACE — LONDON c. 1668		ROBERT DAWE — EXETER c. 1670 – 1711	
AQUILA DACKCOMBE — LONDON 1744 – 1773		THOMAS DEACON — LONDON 1676 – 1685	
ROBERT DAKEN — LONDON 1699		ROBERT DEANE — LONDON 1700 – d. 1713	

WILLIAM DEAN — LONDON 1736		THOMAS DODSON — LONDON 1772	
WILLIAM DE JERSEY — LONDON 1755 – 1785		ERASMUS DOLE — BRISTOL c. 1680 – 1697	
JOHN DE ST. CROIX — LONDON 1729		JOHN DOLE — BRISTOL c. 1700 – 1730	
THOMAS DICKINSON — LONDON 1665		JOHN DONNE — LONDON 1685 – 1727	
WILLIAM DIGGES — LONDON 1699		JOSEPH DONNE — LONDON 1728	
WILLIAM DITCH — LONDON 1668 – c. 1680		RICHARD DONNE — LONDON 1677 – 1696	
EDWARD DODD — LONDON 1672		JOHN DOVE — LONDON 1677 – 1688	

EDWARD
DREW
—
LONDON
1729 – 1764

RICHARD
DRINKWATER
—
LONDON
1713 – 1725

TIMOTHY
DRINKWATER
—
LONDON
1669 – c. 1685

PETER
DUFFIELD
—
LONDON
1647 – 1689

SAMUEL
DUNCOMB
—
BIRMINGHAM
c. 1740 – 1780

JONAS
DURAND
—
LONDON
1699

JOHN
DYER
—
LONDON
1686 – 1715

LAWRENCE
DYER
—
LONDON
1649 – 1698

LAWRENCE
DYER
—
LONDON
1712 – 1726

RICHARD
DYER
—
LONDON
1699

WILLIAM
DYMOCKE
—
LONDON
1696

WILLIAM
EDDON (EDEN)
—
LONDON
1690 – 1733

JAMES
EDGAR
—
EDINBURGH
1709

ROBERT
EDGAR
—
EDINBURGH
1684

THOMAS EDGAR — EDINBURGH 1654	WILLIAM ELLIS — LONDON 1702 – 1729
EDGAR & SON — BRISTOL c. 1814 – 1850	WILLIAM ELLIS — LONDON 1728
JOHN EDWARDS — LONDON 1721	WILLIAM ELLWOOD — LONDON 1696 – 1733
JOHN EDWARDS — LONDON 1753	THOMAS ELPHICK — LONDON 1668 – c. 1675
JOHN ELDERTON — LONDON 1694 – 1745	HENRY ELWICK — LONDON 1723
BARTHOLOMEW ELLIOTT — LONDON 1738 – 1746	JOHN EMES Sr. — LONDON 1675 – 1700
SAMUEL ELLIS — LONDON 1721 – 1749	JOHN EMES Jr. — LONDON 1700 (dated '86)

WILLIAM J. ENGLEFIELD — LONDON 1890 – 1910		WILLIAM FARMER — LONDON 1767 – 1795	
GEORGE EVERARD — LONDON 1676		JOHN FASSON — LONDON 1731 – 1769	
JAMES EVERETT — LONDON 1714		JOHN FASSON — LONDON 1753 – 1796	
JAMES EXCELL — LONDON 1722		THOMAS FASSON — LONDON 1783 – 1844	
SAMUEL FACER — LONDON 1675 – 1687		WILLIAM FASSON — LONDON 1758 – 1800	
JOSHUA FAIRHALL — LONDON 1684 – 1700		FASSON & SONS — LONDON 1784 – 1810	
WILLIAM FARMER — LONDON 1744		THOMAS FAULKNER — LONDON 1679 – 1712	

HENRY
FEILD (FIELD)
—
LONDON
1696

ROBERT
FINDLAY
—
EDINBURGH
1703 – 1730

HENRY
FIELDAR
(FIELDER)
—
LONDON
1710 – 1728

PAUL
FISHER
—
LONDON
1799 – 1819

WILLIAM
FENWICK
—
LONDON
1707 – c. 1715

RICHARD
FLETCHER
—
LONDON
1678 – 1707

ALEXANDER
FERGUSON
—
EDINBURGH
1664 – 1688

FLY &
THOMPSON
—
LONDON
1737 – c. 1745

ALEXANDER
FERGUSON
—
EDINBURGH
1675

JOHN
FERGUSON
—
EDINBURGH
1678

TIMOTHY
FLY
—
LONDON
1712 – 1737

JAMES
FIDDES
—
LONDON
1764 – 1769

WILLIAM
FLY
—
LONDON
1679 – 1697

JAMES
FONTAINE
—
LONDON
1752

ABRAHAM
FORD
—
LONDON
1719 – 1725

GARRAD
FORD
—
WIGAN
c. 1660 – 1694

GILBERT
FORD
—
WIGAN
c. 1670 – 1675

BENJAMIN
FOSTER
—
LONDON
1706 – 1727

BENJAMIN
FOSTER
—
LONDON
1730 – 1748

JOHN
FOSTER
—
LONDON
1741

JOSEPH
FOSTER
—
LONDON
1782

WILLIAM
FOSTER
—
LONDON
1683

THOMAS
FOUNTAIN
—
LONDON
1627 – 1685

WILLIAM
FOX
—
LONDON
1646 – 1675

WILLIAM
FOXON
—
LONDON
1731

PHILIP
FOY
—
EXETER
c. 1720 – 1730

JOHN FRANCIS — LONDON 1663 – c. 1681		WILLIAM FROOME — LONDON 1760	
HENRY FREEMAN — LONDON 1668 – 1687		SIR JOHN FRYERS — LONDON 1693	
ALEXANDER FRENCH — LONDON 1661 – 1684		JOHN GARDINER — LONDON 1764 – 1793	
JOHN FRENCH — LONDON 1630 – 1677		RICHARD GARDINER — LONDON 1670 – 1680	
JOHN FRENCH — LONDON 1687 – 1698		THOMAS GARDINER — LONDON 1682 – 1686	
HENRY FRITH — LONDON 1675		PATRICK GARIOCH — LONDON 1737	
THOMAS FRITH — LONDON 1702 – d. 1713		WILLIAM GARMENTIN — EDINBURGH 1613	

FRANCIS GIBBONS — LONDON 1665 – c. 1685		EVERARD GILLAM — LONDON 1706 – 1714	
JAMES GIBBS — LONDON 1745		WILLIAM GILLAM — LONDON 1698	
WILLIAM GIBBS — LONDON 1806		JAMES GISBURNE — LONDON 1706	
EDWARD GIBSON — EDINBURGH 1719		JOHN GISBURNE — LONDON 1696	
THOMAS GIFFIN — LONDON 1713 – 1759		ROBERT GISBURNE — LONDON 1667	
THOMAS GIFFIN — LONDON 1764 – 1777		JAMES GLAZEBROOK — LONDON 1676	

GEORGE GLEDSTANE — **EDINBURGH** 1610		**EDWARD GOODMAN** — **LONDON** 1669 – 1695	
JOHN GLOVER — **EDINBURGH** 1737 – 1779		**HARRY GOODMAN** — **LONDON** 1694 – 1704	
NICHOLAS GOBLE — **LONDON** 1682		**THOMAS GOODWIN** — **LONDON** 1710 – 1716	
JOSEPH HENRY GODFREY — **LONDON** 1810		**THOMAS GOSLING** — **LONDON** 1725 – 1742	
RICHARD GOING — **BRISTOL** c. 1715 – 1765		**BASILL GRAHAM** — **LONDON** 1699 – 1713	
JOSEPH GOLDIE — **EDINBURGH** 1633		**ALEXANDER GRAHAME** — **EDINBURGH** 1655	

GRA ENGLISH PEWTER TOUCHMARKS

RICHARD
GRAY
—
LONDON
1683

JOHN
GREENWOOD
—
LONDON
1670

GRAY & KING
—
LONDON
1719

THOMAS
GREENWOOD
—
LONDON
1762

JOHN GRAY
GREEN
—
LONDON
1794 – 1803

ROBERT
GREGG
—
LONDON
1673 – 1690

WILLIAM
GREEN
—
LONDON
1678

EDWARD
GREGORY
—
BRISTOL
c. 1680 – 1695
Same mark used
by EDWARD
GREGORY Jr.
up to c. 1730 – 1735

WILLIAM
SANDYS
GREEN
—
LONDON
1729 – 1738

DANIEL
GRENDON
—
LONDON
1736

THOMAS
GREENER
—
LONDON
1702

GEORGE
GRENFELL
—
LONDON
1757 – 1775

JOHN GRIER — EDINBURGH 1702	EDWARD GROVE — LONDON 1677
JOHN GRIFFITH — BRISTOL c. 1745 – 1755	GABRIEL GRUNWIN — LONDON 1684 – 1693
SAMUEL GRIGG — LONDON 1737	RICHARD GRUNWIN — LONDON 1713 – 1726
JOHN GRIMSTED — LONDON 1679 – d. 1685	JOHN GULD — EDINBURGH 1677
THOMAS GROCE — LONDON 1737	JOHN GURNELL — LONDON 1772
WILLIAM GROOME — 1803 – 1815	SAMUEL GUY — LONDON 1730

STEPHEN
HAGGER
—
LONDON
1768

GEORGE
HALE
—
LONDON
1675 – 1680

SIMON
HALFORD
—
LONDON
1730 – 1743

CHARLES
HALIFAX
—
LONDON
1669 – 1685

WILLIAM
HALL
—
LONDON
1668

WILLIAM
HALL
—
LONDON
1680

WILLIAM
HALL
—
LONDON
1687

JOHN
HAMBERLIN
—
LONDON
c. 1671

ALEXANDER
HAMILTON
—
LONDON
1728 – 1755

WILLIAM
HAMILTONE
—
EDINBURGH
1614

JOHN
HAMLIN
—
LONDON
1679

HENRY
HAMMERTON
—
LONDON
1707 – d. 1741

GEORGE
HAMMOND
—
LONDON
1693

SAMUELL
HANCOCK
—
LONDON
1682 – 1713

EDWARD
HANDS
—
LONDON
1705

RICHARD
HANDS
—
LONDON
1728

ROBERT
HANDS
—
LONDON
1682 – 1718

WILLIAM
HANDY
—
LONDON
1737 – d. 1773

JOHN
HANKINSON
—
LONDON
1697

ROBERT
HARDING
—
LONDON
1667 – 1678

HENRY
HARFORD
—
LONDON
1683 – 1706

JABEZ
HARRIS
—
LONDON
1697 – 1706

JOHN
HARRIS
—
LONDON
1709 – 1721

WILLIAM
HARRIS
—
LONDON
1754

JOHN
HARRISON
—
YORK
c. 1689 – 1690

WILLIAM
HARRISON
—
LONDON
1748

GABRIEL
HARTWELL
—
LONDON
1679 – 1686

HENRY
HARTWELL
—
LONDON
1667 – d. 1677

JOHN
HARTWELL
—
LONDON
1747 – d. 1753

JOHN
HARVIE
—
EDINBURGH
1643

JAMES
HARVIE
—
EDINBURGH
1654

WILLIAM
HARVIE
—
EDINBURGH
1672

WILLIAM
HARVIE
—
EDINBURGH
1707

HENRY
HATCH
—
LONDON
1678 – 1681

JOHN
HATHAWAY
—
LONDON
1726 – 1752

THOMAS
HAWARD
—
LONDON
1664 – d. 1674

THOMAS
HAWARD , Jr.
—
LONDON
1664 – 1683

THOMAS
HAWKINS
—
LONDON
1757 – 1765

JOHN
HAYTON
—
LONDON
1745 – 1749

PAUL
HAYTON
—
LONDON
1676

JAMES
HERNIE
—
EDINBURGH
1651

WILLIAM
HEALEY
—
LONDON
1752

JAMES
HERRING
—
EDINBURGH
1669

JOHN
HEANEY
—
DUBLIN
c. 1767 – 1798

JAMES
HERRING
—
EDINBURGH
1686

JOHN
HEATH
—
LONDON
1695 – 1706

JAMES
HERRING
—
EDINBURGH
1692

JOHN
HEATH
—
LONDON
1721

WILLIAM
HERRING
—
EDINBURGH
1693

RICHARD
HEATH
—
LONDON
1671 – 1715

RICHARD
HESLOPP
—
LONDON
1706 – 1735

WILLIAM
HEATON
—
LONDON
1686 – 1706

WILLIAM
HEYFORD
—
LONDON
1699

DAVID
HEYRICK
—
LONDON
1676 – c. 1700

THOMAS
HICKLING
—
LONDON
1676 – 1712

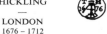

THOMAS
HICKLING
—
LONDON
1720

THOMAS
HICKS
—
LONDON
1670 – 1699

JOSEPH
HIGDON
—
LONDON
1677 – 1685

WILLIAM
HIGHMORE
—
LONDON
1741

SAMUEL
HIGLEY
—
LONDON
1775

JOHN
HINDE
—
LONDON
1772 – d. 1798

WILLIAM
HITCHINS
—
LONDON
1709 – 1736

WILLIAM
HITCHINS
—
LONDON
1760 but dated
1709

JAMES
HITCHMAN
—
LONDON
1701 – 1736

ROBERT
HITCHMAN
—
LONDON
1737 – 1763

RICHARD
HOARE
—
LONDON
1664 – 1693

ROBERT P.
HODGE
—
LONDON
1772 – 1807

EDWARD
HODGKINS , Jr.
—
LONDON
1670 – d. 1680

JOSEPH
HOPKINS
—
LONDON
1663 – 1680

THOMAS
HODGSON
—
LONDON
1676

THOMAS
HORROD
—
LONDON
1704

JOHN
HOLLEY
—
LONDON
1689 – 1706

WILLIAM
HORTON
—
LONDON
1728

EDWARD
HOLMAN
—
LONDON
1689

WILLIAM
HOWARD
—
LONDON
1672–1702

GEORGE
HOLMES
—
LONDON
1743 – 1752

WILLIAM
HOWARD
—
LONDON
1746 – 1758

JOHN
HOME
—
LONDON
1754 – 1777

JOHN
HUDSON
—
LONDON
1771 – d. 1829

THOMAS
HOPKINS
—
LONDON
1701

JAMES
HUGHES
—
LONDON
1692

JOHN HULL — LONDON 1676 -- 1706		THOMAS HUNT — LONDON 1671	
RALPH HULL — LONDON 1656 – 1679		ALEXANDER HUNTER — EDINBURGH 1682	
RALPH HULL — LONDON struck in 1671		WILLIAM HUNTER — EDINBURGH 1749 – 1775	
WILLIAM HULLS — LONDON c. 1699		NICHOLAS HUNTON — LONDON 1662 – 1686	
WILLIAM HULLS — LONDON 1718 – d. 1768		NICHOLAS HUNTON — LONDON struck c. 1670	
CHARLES HULSE — LONDON 1690		WILLIAM HUNTON — LONDON 1683	
GEORGE HUME — LONDON 1702		WILLIAM HURST — LONDON 1677 – d. 1685	

THOMAS
HUX
—
LONDON
1723 – 1763

WILLIAM
HUX
—
LONDON
1700 – 1729

HUMPHREY
HYATT
—
LONDON
1675 – 1684

SOLOMON
IEMPSON
(JEMPSON?)
—
LONDON
1696

EDWARD
ILES
—
LONDON
1675 – 1713

ROBERT
ILES
—
LONDON
1695 – d. 1735

ARTHUR
INGLES
—
LONDON
1711

JONATHAN
INGLES
—
LONDON
struck in 1670

JONATHAN
INGLES
—
LONDON
1671 – 1702
struck in 1671

SAMUEL
INGLES
—
LONDON
1671

ARCHIBALD
INGLIS
—
EDINBURGH
1732 – d. 1773

ROBERT
INGLIS
—
EDINBURGH
1663

THOMAS
INGLIS*
—
EDINBURGH
1616

THOMAS
INGLIS*
*Same man
—
EDINBURGH
1616

THOMAS INGLIS** — EDINBURGH 1648 – d. 1668		HENRY JACKSON — LONDON 1723 – 1743	
THOMAS INGLIS** **Same man* — EDINBURGH 1648 – d. 1668		JOHN JACKSON — LONDON 1677 – 1723	
THOMAS INGLIS — EDINBURGH 1686		JOHN JACKSON — LONDON 1734 – 1743	
THOMAS INGLIS — EDINBURGH 1719 – d. 1732		ROBERT JACKSON — LONDON 1785 – 1801	
DANIEL INGOLE — LONDON 1658 – d. 1691		SAMUEL JACKSON — LONDON 1691 – d. 1715	
HENRY IRVING — LONDON 1750		WILLIAM JACKSON — LONDON 1668 – 1687	
NICHOLAS JACKMAN — LONDON 1703 – 1739		RICHARD JACOB — LONDON 1669	

ROBERT
JACOMB
—
LONDON
1675 – 1686

JOHN
(JOSIAH?)
JACOMBE
—
LONDON
1666 – 1689

ANTHONY
JAMES
—
LONDON
1683 – 1701

LEWIS
JAMES
—
LONDON
1670

RICHARD
JAMES
—
LONDON
1709

THOMAS
JAMES
—
LONDON
1726

JOSEPH
JEFFERYS
—
LONDON
1760

SAMUEL
JEFFERYS
—
LONDON
1735 – 1750

ANTHONY
JENNER
—
LONDON
1767

THEODORE
JENNINGS
—
LONDON
1713 – d. 1749

JOHNSON &
CHAMBERLAIN
—
LONDON
1734

LUKE
JOHNSON
—
LONDON
1723 – 1734

NICHOLAS
JOHNSON
—
LONDON
1679 – 1731

ROBERT
JONES
—
LONDON
1657 – 1678

WILLIAM
JOHNSON
—
LONDON
1681

SETH
JONES
—
LONDON
1719 – 1746

JOHN
JOLLY
—
EDINBURGH
1714

THOMAS
JONES
—
LONDON
1760

CHARLES
JONES
—
LONDON
1791 – 1796

JOHN
JORDAN
—
LONDON
1727

HENRY
JONES
—
LONDON
1675 – 1680

HENRY
JOSEPH
—
LONDON
1740 – 1785

JOHN
JONES
—
LONDON
1700 – 1745

HENRY &
RICHARD
JOSEPH
—
LONDON
1787 – 1815

JOHN
JONES
—
LONDON
1727 – d. 1783

JOHN
JOYCE
—
LONDON
1683 – 1690

JOHN JUPE — LONDON 1737 – d. 1781		WILLIAM KENDRICK — LONDON 1677 – 1686	
ROBERT JUPE — LONDON 1704 – d. 1737		EDWARD KENT — LONDON 1683 – 1692	
ROBERT JUPE — LONDON 1780		JOHN KENT — LONDON 1723 – 1759	
NICHOLAS KELK — LONDON c. 1640 – d. 1687		JOHN KENTON — LONDON 1677 – 1722	
THOMAS KELK — LONDON 1678		JOHN KENTON — LONDON struck in 1692	
ROBERT KELLOWE — EDINBURGH 1715		PETER LE KEUX — LONDON 1794 – 1805	
JOHN KENDRICK — LONDON 1737 – 1744		JOHN KING — LONDON 1761	

JOSEPH
KING
—
LONDON
1683

ANDREW
KINNEAR
—
EDINBURGH
1750 – 1793

RICHARD
KING
—
LONDON
1722 – d. 1757

THOMAS
KIRBY
—
LONDON
1729

RICHARD
KING
—
LONDON
1722 – d. 1757

THOMAS
KIRKE
—
LONDON
1728

RICHARD
KING , Jr.
—
LONDON
1707 – 1738

JOHN
KIRTON
—
LONDON
1702

THOMAS
KING
—
LONDON
1675 – 1708

FRANCIS
KNIGHT
—
LONDON
1680 – 1692

WILLIAM
KING
—
LONDON
c. 1706

JAMES
KNIGHT
—
LONDON
1676 – 1698

WILLIAM H.
KING
—
LONDON
1786 – c. 1830

ROBERT KNIGHT — LONDON 1785	
SAMUEL KNIGHT — LONDON 1712	
JOHN LAFFAR — LONDON 1711 – 1720	
ALEXANDER LANCASTER — LONDON 1725	
EDWARD LANE — LONDON 1671	
JOHN LANGFORD — LONDON 1720 – d. 1757	

THOMAS LANGFORD — LONDON 1755	
ADAM LANGLEY — LONDON 1658 – 1687	
JOHN LANGLEY — LONDON 1720	
JOHN LANGTON — LONDON 1736 – d. 1757	
WILLIAM LANSDOWN — BRISTOL c. 1740 – d. 1761	
THOMAS LANYON — BRISTOL 1715 – 1755	

JOHN
LAUGHTON
—
LONDON
1678

STEPHEN
LAWRENCE
—
LONDON
1662 – 1691

JOHN
LAUGHTON
—
LONDON
struck in 1692

STEPHEN
LAWRENCE
—
LONDON
1708

JOHN
LAW
—
EDINBURGH
1658

DANIEL
LAWSON
—
LONDON
1749 – 1758

SAMUEL
LAW
—
LONDON
1770

JOHN
LAWSON
—
LONDON
1714 – 1749

EDWARD
LAWRANCE
—
LONDON
1713 – 1727

FRANCIS
LEA
—
LONDON
c. 1653 – 1675
restruck c. 1668

JOHN
LAWRANCE
—
LONDON
1686 – 1726

FRANCIS
LEA
—
LONDON
restruck c. 1668

FRANCIS
LEA
—
LONDON
restruck c. 1668

JONATHAN
LEACH
—
LONDON
1746 – 1769

THOMAS
LEACH
—
LONDON
1678 – 1691

THOMAS
LEACH
—
LONDON
1721 – 1745

EDWARD
LEAPIDGE
—
LONDON
1699 – 1727

THOMAS
LEAPIDGE
—
LONDON
1692 – d. 1699

JOHN
LEESON
—
LONDON
1646 – 1684

JOHN
LEESON
—
LONDON
1675 – 1690

RICHARD
LEGGATT
—
LONDON
1727 – 1746

JOHN
LETHAM
—
EDINBURGH
1718 – d. 1756

JAMES
LETHARD
—
LONDON
1746

WILLIAM
LEWIS
—
LONDON
c. 1668

JOHN
LILLEY
—
LONDON
c. 1671

THOMAS
LINCOLNE
—
LONDON
1719 – 1739

71

GREENHILL
LINDSEY
—
LONDON
1711 – 1723

FRANCIS
LITCHFIELD
—
LONDON
1700

HENRY
LITTLE
—
LONDON
1737 – d. 1764

CHARLES W.
LOADER
—
LONDON
1784 – 1798

JEREMIAH
LOADER
—
LONDON
1668 – 1686

ROBERT
LOCK
—
LONDON
1678 – d. 1706

THOMAS
LOCK
—
LONDON
1684

EDWARD
LOCKWOOD
—
LONDON
1785 – 1819

WILLIAM
LONG
—
LONDON
1684 – 1707

JOHN
LOVELL
—
BRISTOL
1725 – 1744
Same mark used,
with label of
ROBERT
LOVELL,
until *c.* 1760

ROBERT
LUCAS
—
LONDON
1641 – 1677

ROBERT
LUPTON
—
LONDON
1781

STEPHEN
MABBERLEY
—
LONDON
1771 – d. 1784

SAMUEL
MABBS
—
LONDON
1677 – d. 1697

ANDREW
McCLEAN
—
EDINBURGH
1659

GILES
MADGWICK
—
LONDON
1681

NICHOLAS
MARRIOTT
—
LONDON
1687 – c. 1713

JOHN
MARSH
—
LONDON
1682

RALPH
MARSH Jnr.
—
LONDON
1665 – c. 1685

THOMAS
MARSHALL
—
LONDON
1684

ROBERT
MARTIN
—
LONDON
1638 – d. 1674

WILLIAM
MARTIN
—
LONDON
1726

DANIEL
MASON
—
LONDON
1672 – d. 1682

ROBERT
MASSAM
—
LONDON
1736 – 1755

RICHARD
MASTEAD
—
LONDON
1668 – 1700

EDWARD
MATTHEWS
—
LONDON
1691 – 1704

JAMES
MATTHEWS
—
LONDON
1724

PHILLIP
MATTHEWS
—
LONDON
1736 – 1755

ROBERT
MATTHEWS
—
LONDON
1727

THOMAS
MATTHEWS
—
LONDON
1716 – 1744

THOMAS
MATTHEWS, Jr.
—
LONDON
1741 – 1750

WILLIAM
MATTHEWS, Sr.
—
LONDON
1674 – d. 1691

WILLIAM
MATTHEWS, Jr.
—
LONDON
1698

JOHN H.
MAW
—
LONDON
1822 – 1847

CHARLES P.
MAXEY
—
LONDON
1750

HENRY
MAXTED
—
LONDON
1735

JOSIAH
MAYNARD
—
LONDON
1796

ANTHONY
MAYORS
—
LONDON
1648 – d. 1677

WILLIAM
MEADOWS
—
LONDON
1716

NATHANIEL
MEAKIN Jr.
—
LONDON
1762 – 1783

RICHARD
MEDDOWS
—
LONDON
1673 – 1686

WILLIAM
MILES
—
LONDON
1716 – 1725

EDWARD
MERIEFIELD
—
LONDON
1724 – 1744

WILLIAM
MILLIN
—
LONDON
1782 – 1801

JOHN MERRI-
WEATHER
—
LONDON
1719 – 1728

JONATHAN
MILLMAN
—
LONDON
c. 1680

JOHN C.
MERRI-
WEATHER
—
LONDON
1749 – 1765

NATHANIEL
MILLS
—
LONDON
1640 – c. 1675

CHARLES
MIDDLETON
—
LONDON
1695 – 1700

RICHARD
MISTER
—
LONDON
1802 – d. 1839

THOMAS
MIDDLETON
—
LONDON
1673

PAUL
MITCHELL
—
LONDON
1723 – 1741

SAMUEL
MILES
—
LONDON
1726

THOMAS
MITCHELL
—
EDINBURGH
1705

ALEXANDER MOIR — EDINBURGH 1672		ROBERT MORSE — LONDON 1706 – 1713	
JOSEPH MONK — LONDON 1771		ROGER MOSER — LONDON 1807	
JAMES MONTEITH — EDINBURGH 1634		THOMAS MORTON — LONDON c. 1673	
JAMES MONTEITH — EDINBURGH 1643		PETER MOULESWORTH — LONDON 1683 – 1693	
RANDAL MORING — LONDON 1780 – 1821		JOSEPH MOUNTFORD — LONDON 1685	
WILLIAM MORS — LONDON 1678 ·		THOMAS MUNDAY — LONDON 1758 – 1790	
HENRY MORSE — LONDON 1676		MUNDEN & GROVE — LONDON 1760 – 1773	
ROBERT MORSE — LONDON 1677			

WILLIAM MURRAY — LONDON 1735 – 1743	EDWARD NEWBOULT — LONDON 1668 – 1675
ARCHIBALD NAPIER — EDINBURGH 1666	SAMUEL NEWELL — LONDON 1695
JOHN NAPIER — EDINBURGH 1700	JOHN NEWHAM — LONDON 1700 – 1733
HENRY NAPTON — LONDON 1769 – d. 1784	WILLIAM NEWHAM — LONDON 1712 – 1745
EDWARD NASH — LONDON 1720 – 1735	RICHARD NEWMAN — LONDON 1747 – 1780
JOHN NEATON — LONDON 1715	JAMES NICHOLLS Sr. — LONDON 1652 – d. 1686
WILLIAM NETTLEFOLD — LONDON 1800 – 1817	JAMES NICHOLLS Jr. — LONDON 1686

WILLIAM
NICHOLLS
—
LONDON
1685 – 1705

NICHOLAS
OKEFORD
—
LONDON
1702 – 1732

ROBERT
NICHOLSON
—
LONDON
1687 – 1732

JOHN
OLIVER
—
LONDON
1685 – 1692

WILLIAM
NICHOLSON
—
LONDON
1721 – 1745

WILLIAM
ONLY
—
LONDON
1675 – 1687

RICHARD
NORFOLK
—
LONDON
1741 – 1779

CHARLES
OSBORN
—
LONDON
1684

JOHN
NORGROVE
—
LONDON
1726

JOHN
OSBORN
—
LONDON
1712 – 1733

GEORGE
NORTH
—
LONDON
1697 – 1725

JOHN
OSBORN
—
LONDON
1721 – 1758

WILLIAM
NORWOOD
—
LONDON
1727

JOHN
OSBORN
—
LONDON
1785

ROBERT OUDLEY — LONDON 1709 – 1732			DANIEL PARKER — LONDON 1686 – 1714	
JOHN PAGE — LONDON 1692 – 1700			JOSEPH PARKER — LONDON 1670 – 1687	
THOMAS PAGE — BRISTOL c. 1737 – 1745			THOMAS PARKER — LONDON 1700	
JOHN PALMER —. LONDON 1714			THOMAS PARKER — LONDON 1700	
THOMAS PALMER — LONDON 1689			JOHN PARKINSON — LONDON 1683	
WILLIAM PALMER — LONDON 1744 – 1751			NORTON PARR — CORK c. 1740 – d. 1773	
FRANCIS PARADICE — LONDON 1678 – d. 1709			ROBERT PARR — LONDON 1703 – d. 1777	

RICHARD
PARTRIDGE
—
LONDON
1715 – 1724

WILLIAM
PAXTON
—
LONDON
1670 – d. 1706

WALTER
PATASON
—
EDINBURGH
1710

JOHN
PAYNE
—
LONDON
1728

ROBERT
PATIENCE
—
LONDON
1737 – d. 1777

JOHN
PAYNELL
—
LONDON
1677

SIMON
PATTINSON
—
LONDON
1723 – d. 1768

JOHN
PEACOCK
—
LONDON
1709 – c. 1735

RICHARD
PAWSON
—
LONDON
1753 – 1765

RICHARD
PEAKE
—
LONDON
1751

JAMES
PAXTON
—
LONDON
1706 – 1725

JOSEPH
PEDDER
—
LONDON
1729

JOHN
PAXTON
—
LONDON
1724 – 1729

ROBERT
PEIRCY
—
LONDON
1735 – d. 1766

GEORGE
PEISLEY
—
LONDON
1718 – 1729

FRANCIS
PERKINS
—
LONDON
1680

THOMAS
PEISLEY
—
LONDON
1708 – 1718

RICHARD
PERKINS
—
BRISTOL
c. 1770 – 1780

THOMAS
PEISLEY
—
LONDON
1710 – 1718

JOHN
PERRY
—
LONDON
1743 – 1777

DAVID
PENMAN
—
EDINBURGH
1693 – d. 1715

JOHN
PERRY
—
LONDON
1765 – d. 1818

HUMPHREY
PENN
—
LONDON
1677

JOHN
PETTIT
—
LONDON
1685 – 1713

JOHN
PEPPER
—
LONDON
1678 – 1688

JOHN
PETTIVER
—
LONDON
1680 – d. 1698

HELLIER
PERCHARD
—
LONDON
1709 – d. 1759

SAMUEL
PETTIVER
—
LONDON
1704 – d. 1724

WILLIAM PETTIVER — LONDON 1655 – 1680		**WILLIAM PHIPPS** — LONDON 1750	
WILLIAM PETTIVER — LONDON 1679 – 1686		**JOSEPH PICKARD** — LONDON 1693 – 1708	
THOMAS PHILLIPS — LONDON 1729	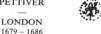	**DANIEL PICKERING** — LONDON 1727	
THOMAS PHILLIPS — LONDON 1800		**THOMAS PICKFAT** — LONDON 1680 – 1686	
WILLIAM PHILLIPS — LONDON 1730 – 1739	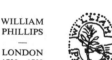	**JOSEPH PIDDEL** — LONDON 1684 – 1692	
WILLIAM PHILLIPS — LONDON 1750		**TRISTRAM PIERCE** — LONDON 1702	
WILLIAM PHILLIPS — LONDON 1773 – 1793		**FRANCIS PIGGOTT** — LONDON 1738 – 1773	

JOHN
PIGGOTT
—
LONDON
1736 – 1754

THOMAS
PIGGOTT
—
LONDON
1725

ROBERT
PILKINGTON
—
LONDON
1705 – 1716

PITT &
DADLEY
—
LONDON
1781 – 1797

PITT & FLOYD
—
LONDON
1769 – 1780

RICHARD
PITT
—
LONDON
1747 – 1770

JOSEPH
PIXLEY
—
LONDON
c. 1708

WILLIAM
PLIVEY
—
LONDON
1698

ROBERT
POLE
—
LONDON
1719

RICHARD
POOLE
—
LONDON
1748

ROWLAND
POOLE
—
LONDON
1724

LUKE
PORTER
—
LONDON
1679

THOMAS
PORTER
—
LONDON
1683 – d. 1706

ROBERT
PORTEUS
—
LONDON
1762 – 1790

THOMAS
POWELL
—
LONDON
1681 – d. 1723

HENRY
PRATT
—
LONDON
1675

JOSEPH
PRATT
—
LONDON
1672 – 1709

JOSEPH
PRATT
—
LONDON
1721

SAMUEL
PRIDDLE
—
LONDON
1780

PETER
PRIEST
—
LONDON
1667 – 1676

JOHN
PRINCE
—
LONDON
1701 – 1713

JAMES
PULESTON
—
LONDON
1759

EDWARD
PUSEY
—
LONDON
1678

ROGER
PYE
—
LONDON
1738 – 1784

EDWARD
QUICK Sr.
—
LONDON
1687 – 1707

EDWARD
QUICK
—
LONDON
1709 – 1728

EDWARD
QUICK Jr.
—
LONDON
1741 – d. 1773

HUGH
QUICK
—
LONDON
1674 – 1729

JOHN
QUICK
—
LONDON
1701

SAMUEL
QUISSEN-
BOROUGH
—
LONDON
1673 – 1693

CHARLES
RACK
—
LONDON
1681 – 1691

THOMAS
RADCLIFF
—
LONDON
1672

JAMES
RAIT
—
EDINBURGH
1718

JOHN
RAMSAY
—
EDINBURGH
1659

CHARLES
RANDALL
—
LONDON
1700

EDWARD
RANDALL
—
LONDON
1679 – 1711

EDWARD
RANDALL
—
LONDON
1714

JOHN
RANDALL
—
LONDON
1723 – 1731

ROBERT
RANDALL
—
LONDON
1751

CHRISTOPHER
RAPER
—
LONDON
1669 – 1692

WILLIAM
RAVES
—
LONDON
1699

JOHN
RAWLINSON
—
LONDON
1675

JOSEPH
RAYNE
—
LONDON
1696

ISAAC
READ
—
LONDON
1749 – 1757

PETER
REDKNAP
—
LONDON
1713 – 1736

ROGER
READING
—
LONDON
1670 – 1690

JOHN
REDSHAW
—
LONDON
1681 – 1699

THEOPHILUS
READING
—
LONDON
1676 – 1688

ISAAC
REEVE
—
LONDON
1755 – d. 1796

THEOPHILUS
READING
—
LONDON
1688

ROBERT
REID
—
EDINBURGH
1718

JOHN
REBATE
—
EDINBURGH
1588

EDWARD
RELFE
—
LONDON
1672 – 1686

ANTHONY
REDHEAD
—
LONDON
1676 – 1714

CHARLES
RENDER
—
LONDON
1700

GABRIEL
REDHEAD
—
LONDON
1664 – c. 1700

JOHN
REYNOLDS
—
LONDON
1696

ROBERT REYNOLDS — LONDON 1704		SAMUEL RIGHTON — LONDON 1734 – 1743	
THOMAS RHODES — LONDON 1721 – 1754		ABRAHAM ROBERTS — LONDON 1704	
TIMOTHY RICHARDS — LONDON 1707 – 1719		EDWARD ROBERTS — LONDON 1686	
WILLIAM RICHARDS — LONDON 1671		PHILLIP ROBERTS — LONDON 1738 – 1746	
THOMAS RIDDING — LONDON 1674 – 1692		THOMAS ROBERTS — LONDON 1688 – d. 1703	
THOMAS RIDDING — LONDON 1705		OBEDIENCE ROBINS — LONDON 1675 – d. 1712	
NATHANIEL RIDER — LONDON 1679		JOHN ROBINSON — LONDON 1670	

THOMAS
RODWELL
—
YORK
c. 1704 – 1730

WILLIAM
ROWELL
—
LONDON
1727 – 1735

JOHN
ROGERS
—
LONDON
1725

CHARLES
ROYCE
—
LONDON
1686

PHILLIP
ROGERS
—
LONDON
1708

PHILIP
RUDDUCK
—
LONDON
1692

ANTHONY
ROLLS
—
LONDON
1646 – 1669

ANDREW
RUDSBY
—
LONDON
1679 – d. 1715

JOHN
ROLT
—
LONDON
1718 – d. 1727

ANDREW
RUDSBY
—
LONDON
1728

GEORGE
ROOKE
—
LONDON
1668 – d. 1673

JOHN
RUSSELL
—
LONDON
1676

JOHN
ROTHWELL
—
LONDON
1671 – d. 1681

JOSEPH
SANDFORD
—
LONDON
1674

WILLIAM
SANDYS
—
LONDON
struck in 1680

WILLIAM
SAYER
—
LONDON
1706 – 1715

WILLIAM
SANDYS
—
LONDON
1692 – d. 1713

ROBERT
SAYERS
—
LONDON
1669 – d. 1711

HUMPHREY
SANKEY
—
LONDON
1710

ROBERT
SCATCHARD
—
LONDON
1758 – 1771

THOMAS
SAUNDERS
—
LONDON
1684

JOHN
SCATTERGOOD
—
LONDON
1735 – d. 1744

JOHN
SAUNDERS
—
LONDON
1675

THOMAS
SCATTERGOOD
—
LONDON
1703 – d. 1785

JOHN
SAVAGE
—
LONDON
1704

THOMAS
SCATTERGOOD
—
LONDON
1736 – d. 1778

JOHN
SAVIDGE
—
LONDON
1681

GEORGE
SCOTT
—
LONDON
1680 – d. 1716

WILLIAM
SCOTT
—
EDINBURGH
1634

WILLIAM
SCOTT
—
EDINBURGH
1735 – 1779

WILLIAM
SCOTT
—
EDINBURGH
1772

SAMUEL
SEATON
—
LONDON
1683 – 1718

EDWARD
SEAWELL
—
LONDON
1794 – 1801

JOHN
SELLON
—
LONDON
1749

HENRY
SEWDLEY
—
LONDON
1709 – 1740

JOHN
SHAKLE
—
LONDON
1685

THOMAS
SHAKLE Sr.
—
LONDON
1677
Also
THOMAS
SHAKLE Jr.
used this mark
up to 1709

EDMUND
SHARROCK
—
LONDON
1737

JOHN
SHARP
—
LONDON
1692

JOHN
SHAW
—
LONDON
1726

WILLIAM
SHAYLER
—
LONDON
1734 – 1743

SAMUEL
SHEPPARD
—
LONDON
1685

THOMAS
SHEPPARD
—
LONDON
1708 – d. 1729

ALEXANDER
SIBBALD
—
EDINBURGH
1606

JOSEPH
SHERWIN
—
LONDON
1727 – 1736

JAMES
SIBBALD
—
EDINBURGH
1631

WILLIAM
SHERWOOD
—
LONDON
1741

JAMES
SIBBET
—
EDINBURGH
1600

JOHN
SHOREY Sr.
—
LONDON
1683 – 1721

HENRY
SIBLEY
—
LONDON
1682

JOHN
SHOREY Jr.
—
LONDON
1708 – 1732

EDWARD
SIDEY
—
LONDON
1773

NATHANIEL
SHORTGRAVE
—
LONDON
1687

JOHN
SILX
—
LONDON
c. 1630 – 1670

RICHARD
SHURMER
—
LONDON
1680 – 1699

JOHN
SILX
—
LONDON
1693 – 1705

VINCENT
SILK
—
LONDON
1663 – 1670

THOMAS
SIMMS
—
LONDON
1679

ROBERT
SIMPSON
—
EDINBURGH
1633

THOMAS
SIMPSON
—
EDINBURGH
1728 – 1780

JOHN
SKINN
—
LONDON
1670 – d. 1690

THOMAS
SKINN
—
LONDON
1673

ROBERT
SKYNNER
—
LONDON
1738

JOHN
SLOW
—
LONDON
1674 – 1724

JOSEPH
SLOW
—
LONDON
1703

SAMUEL
SMALLEY
—
LONDON
1690 – 1713

ARTHUR
SMALMAN
—
LONDON
1722

RICHARD
SMALPIECE
—
LONDON
1683

ANTHONY
SMITH
—
LONDON
1700

CHARLES
SMITH
—
LONDON
1766 – 1796

EDWARD SMITH — LONDON 1690 – 1703		JOHN SMITH — LONDON 1703 – 1720	
GEORGE SMITH — LONDON 1681 – d. 1695		JOHN SMITH — LONDON 1726 – 1750	
GEORGE SMITH — LONDON 1713 – d. 1762		JOSEPH SMITH — LONDON 1695 – 1707	
HENRY SMITH — LONDON 1726 – d. 1744		RICHARD SMITH — LONDON 1677 – 1709	
JAMES SMITH — LONDON 1733		RICHARD SMITH — LONDON 1735 – 1760	
JOHN SMITH — LONDON 1675		ROWLAND SMITH — LONDON 1750	
JOHN SMITH — LONDON 1685 – 1697		SAMUEL SMITH — LONDON 1727 – 1761	

THOMAS SMITH — LONDON 1675 – 1684		WILLIAM SMITH — LONDON 1669 – 1686	
THOMAS SMITH — LONDON 1682 – 1693		WILLIAM SMITH — LONDON 1692	
THOMAS SMITH — LONDON 1687		WILLIAM SMITH — LONDON 1732	
THOMAS SMITH — LONDON 1706 – 1739		WILLIAM SMITH — YORK 1730	
THOMAS SMITH — LONDON 1760		SMITH & LEAPIDGE — LONDON 1728 – 1750	
THOMAS SMITH — LONDON 1764		WILLIAM SNAPE — LONDON 1767 – d. 1783	
THOMAS SMITH — LONDON 1768		JOHN SNOXELL — LONDON 1675 – 1685	

SPACKMAN & GRANT — LONDON 1709 – 1758		RICHARD SPOONER — LONDON 1723 – 1762	
JOSEPH SPACKMAN — LONDON 1753		PENTLEBURY SPRING — LONDON 1718	
JOSEPH & JAMES SPACKMAN — LONDON 1781		THOMAS SPRING — LONDON 1694	
JOSEPH SPACKMAN & CO. — LONDON 1785 – 1796		GEORGE STAFFORD — LONDON 1730 – 1753	
SAMUEL SPATEMAN — LONDON 1720 – 1729		JAMES STANTON — LONDON 1819 – d. 1835	
THOMAS SPENCER — LONDON 1702		ROBERT STANTON — LONDON 1810 – d. 1842	
JOHN SPICER — LONDON 1705 – 1732		JAMES STEVENS — LONDON 1754 – 1781	

JONATHAN
STEVENS
—
LONDON
1745 – 1756

EDWARD
STONE
—
LONDON
1698

PHILIP
STEVENS
—
LONDON
1709 – 1726

ALEXANDER
STOUT
—
LONDON
1736

THOMAS
STEVENS
—
LONDON
1720 – 1750

JOHN
STRIBBLEHILL
—
LONDON
1678 – 1704

WILLIAM
STEVENS
—
LONDON
1700 – 1722

THOMAS
STRIBBLEHILL
—
LONDON
1724

WILLIAM
STEVENS
—
LONDON
1729 – 1738

JOHN
STRICKLAND
—
LONDON
1716

WILLIAM
STIFF
—
BRISTOL
1763

WALTER
STURT
—
LONDON
1673 – 1690

JOHN
STILES
—
LONDON
1689

ANTHONY
STURTON
—
LONDON
1702 – 1730

ROBERT
STURROP
—
LONDON
1683 – d. 1697

JOHN
SUMMERS
—
LONDON
1697

THOMAS
SWANSON
—
LONDON
struck
1760 – d. 1783

THOMAS
SWANSON
—
LONDON
struck 1765

NICHOLAS
SWEATMAN
—
LONDON
1699 – d. 1721

SAMUEL
SWEATMAN
—
LONDON
1741

CHARLES
SWEETING
—
LONDON
1663 – c. 1680

CORNELIUS
SWIFT
—
LONDON
1777 – 1805

WILLIAM
CORNELIUS
SWIFT
—
LONDON
1827 – d. 1832

THOMAS
SWINDELL
—
LONDON
1727

JOHN
SYDE
—
EDINBURGH
1655

JOHN
SYDE
—
EDINBURGH
1680

DAVID
SYMMER
—
EDINBURGH
1692

JAMES
SYMONTOUN
—
EDINBURGH
1696

ADAM
TAIT
—
EDINBURGH
1747

JAMES
TAYLOR
—
LONDON
1667 – 1675

JOHN
TAIT
—
EDINBURGH
1700

SAMUEL
TAYLOR
—
LONDON
1734 – 1748

RICHARD
TALVER
—
LONDON
1668 – c. 1678

THOMAS
TAYLOR
—
LONDON
1670 – 1716

JAQUES
TAUDIN Sr.
—
LONDON
1657 – d. 1697

WILLIAM
TAYLOR
—
LONDON
c. 1745

JAQUES
TAUDIN Jr.
—
LONDON
1680 – c. 1705

JOHN
TEALE
—
LONDON
1675 – d. 1694

CORNELIUS
TAYLEOUR
—
EDINBURGH
1610

THOMAS
TEMPLEMAN
—
LONDON
1668 – 1713

GEORGE
TAYLOR
—
LONDON
1722

GEORGE
TENNENT
—
EDINBURGH
1706

JOHN
THOMAS
—
LONDON
1698 – 1724

BENEDICTUS
THOMSON
—
LONDON
1673

ROBERT
THOMSON
—
EDINBURGH
1631

THOMAS
THOMSON
—
LONDON
1764

CHRISTOPHER
THORNE
—
LONDON
1675 – 1685

WILLIAM
TIBBING
—
LONDON
1679

ANN
TIDMARSH
—
LONDON
1728

JAMES
TIDMARSH
—
LONDON
1704 – 1731

JAMES
TIDMARSH , Jr.
—
LONDON
1734 – 1750

JOHN
TIDMARSH
—
LONDON
1715 – d. 1765

THOMAS
TIDMARSH
—
LONDON
1677 – 1728

ROBERT
TILLOTT
—
LONDON
1677

THOMAS
TILYARD
—
LONDON
1698 – 1713

JAMES
TISOE Sr.
—
LONDON
1689 – 1757

JAMES
TISOE Jr.
—
LONDON
1734 – d. 1771

EDWARD
TOMS
—
LONDON
1744 – 1783

TOWNSEND &
COMPTON
—
LONDON
1780 – 1811

MATTHEW
TONKIN
—
LONDON
1749 – d. 1755

EDWARD
TRAHERN
—
LONDON
1680

CHARLES
TOUGH
—
LONDON
1687 – 1692

JOHN
TRAPP
—
LONDON
1720

BENJAMIN
TOWNSEND
—
LONDON
1754 – 1778

JAMES
TREW
—
LONDON
1673

JOHN
TOWNSEND
—
LONDON
1748 – d. 1801

JOHN
TROUT
—
LONDON
1689

JOHN
TOWNSEND &
R. REYNOLDS
—
LONDON
1767 – 1788

DAUBENY
TURBERVILLE
—
LONDON
1705 – 1720

WILLIAM
TOWNSEND
—
LONDON
1707

SAMUEL
TURNER
—
LONDON
1801 – c. 1810

WILLIAM TURNER — LONDON 1705	RICHARD VERNON — LONDON 1635 – c. 1670
EDWARD UBLY — LONDON 1721 – 1744	SAMUEL VERNON — LONDON 1674
JOHN UBLY — LONDON 1750	ROBERT VEITCH — EDINBURGH 1725
THOMAS UBLY — LONDON 1741 – 1751	GEORGE VIBART — LONDON 1676
GEORGE UNDERWOOD — LONDON 1712	THOMAS VILE , Sr. — LONDON 1641 – c. 1673
MATTHEW UNDERWOOD — LONDON 1752 – 1761	THOMAS VILE Jr. — LONDON 1667 – c. 1680
JOHN VAUGHAN — LONDON 1759 – d 1807	WILLIAM VINMONT — LONDON 1678 – c. 1690

BARTHOLOMEW
VOKINS
—
LONDON
1670

EDWARD
WALKER
—
LONDON
1683 – 1709

ALEXANDER
WADDEL
—
EDINBURGH
1714 – 1721

JOHN
WALKER
—
LONDON
1714 – 1728

WILLIAM
WADSWORTH
—
LONDON
1789

JOHN
WALKER
—
LONDON
1751

JOHN
WAITE
—
LONDON
1673

PATRICK
WALKER
—
EDINBURGH
1607

JOHN
WAITE
—
LONDON
1712

ROBERT
WALKER
—
EDINBURGH
1676 – d. 1688

THOMAS
WAITE
—
LONDON
1679

SAMUEL
WALKER
—
EDINBURGH
1660

ALEXANDER
WALKER
—
EDINBURGH
1675

WILLIAM
WALKER
—
LONDON
1790 – d. 1849

ROBERT
WALLER
—
LONDON
1782

EDWARD
WALMSLEY
—
LONDON
1688

JOHN
WALMSLEY
—
LONDON
1713

RICHARD
WALTON
—
LONDON
1675

RICHARD
WARKMAN
—
LONDON
1698 – 1703

WILLIAM
WARKMAN
—
LONDON
1721

JOHN
WARREN
—
LONDON
1699 – 1732

LAWRENCE
WARREN
—
LONDON
1672 – d. 1683

ROBERT
WASS
—
LONDON
1723

ANTHONY
WATERS
—
LONDON
1698 – 1720

WILLIAM
WATERS
—
LONDON
1677

WILLIAM
WATKINS
—
BRISTOL
1728

JOHN
WATSON
—
EDINBURGH
1671

JOSEPH
WATSON
—
LONDON
1720

THOMAS
WATTERER
—
LONDON
1681 – 1704

JOHN
WATTS
—
LONDON
1725 – d. 1765

WILLIAM
WAYLETT
—
LONDON
1702

RICHARD
WEBB
—
LONDON
1687

THOMAS
WEBB
—
LONDON
1716 – 1723

JOHN
WEIR
—
EDINBURGH
1584

JOHN
WEIR
—
EDINBURGH
1701

RICHARD
WEIR
—
EDINBURGH
1600

ROBERT
WEIR
—
EDINBURGH
1646

THOMAS
WEIR
—
EDINBURGH
1596

JOHN
WESCOTT
—
LONDON
1670

MOSES
WEST
—
LONDON
1677 – 1696

WILLIAM
WETTER
—
LONDON
c. 1666 – 70

RALPH
WHARRAM
—
LONDON
1762

ARTHUR
WHARTON
—
YORK
1740 – 1758

THOMAS
WHEELER
—
LONDON
1713 – 1735

BANJAMIN
WHITAKER
—
LONDON
1691

DANIEL
WHITE
—
LONDON
1684 – 1699

JOHN
WHITE
—
LONDON
1755 – 1772

JOSEPH
WHITE
—
LONDON
1747 – 1755

PHILLIP
WHITE
—
LONDON
1786

RICHARD
WHITE
—
LONDON
1688 – 1742

WILLIAM
WHITE
—
LONDON
1751 – d. 1783

WHITE &
BERNARD
—
LONDON
1721

FRANCIS
WHITTLE
—
LONDON
1719 – 1740

GEORGE
WHYTE
—
EDINBURGH
1676

JOHN
WIDDOWES
—
LONDON
1671

ABRAHAM
WIGGIN

—

LONDON
1708

EDWARD
WILLETT

—

LONDON
1684 – d. 1743

HENRY
WIGGIN

—

LONDON
1682 – 1693

MARY
WILLEY

—

LONDON
1760

WILLIAM
WIGHTMAN

—

LONDON
1761 – 1801

JOHN
WILLIAMS

LONDON
1678 – 1689

THOMAS
WIGLEY

—

LONDON
1705

JOHN
WILLIAMS

—

LONDON
1729

RICHARD
WILDMAN

—

LONDON
1703

JOHN
WILLIAMS

—

LONDON
1741

RICHARD
WILKS

—

LONDON
1708

ROBERT
WILLIAMS

—

LONDON
1692

ROGER WILLOUGHBY — **BRISTOL** 1680 – d. 1687	**JOSEPH WINGOD** — **LONDON** 1723 – 1763
THOMAS WILLSHIRE — **BRISTOL** 1785 – 1825	**MOSES WINKWORTH** — **LONDON** 1673 – d. 1693
DANIEL WILSON — **LONDON** 1692 – 1702	**GEORGE WINTER** — **LONDON** 1702
JOHN WILSON — **EDINBURGH** 1732	**RICHARD WITHEBED** — **LONDON** 1669 – 1685
THOMAS WINCHCOMBE — **LONDON** 1694 – 1701	**BENJAMIN WITHERS** — **LONDON** 1720 – 1737
JOHN WINGOD — **LONDON** 1749 – d. 1784	**WILLIAM WITHERS** — **LONDON** 1655 – d. 1678
	WILLIAM WITHERS — **LONDON** 1685 – 1725

ELIZABETH
WITTER

—

LONDON
1691 – 1712

SAMUEL
WITTER

—

LONDON
1671 – d. 1691

HENRY
WOOD

—

LONDON
1769 – 1791

ROBERT
WOOD

—

LONDON
1671 – 1722

WOOD & HILL

—

LONDON
1798

WOOD &
MITCHELL

—

LONDON
1742 – 1752

JOHN
WOODESON

—

LONDON
1712 – 1723

F. HUMPHREY
WORMLAYTON

—

LONDON
1701

ALEXANDER
WRIGHT

—

EDINBURGH
1732 – 1773

JOHN
WRIGHT

—

LONDON
1736 – 1743

RICHARD
WRIGHT

—

LONDON
1723

THOMAS
WRIGHT

—

LONDON
1683 – d. 1685

WILLIAM
WRIGHT

—

LONDON
1780 – 1802

JOHN
WYATT

—

LONDON
1687 – 1701

JOHN
WYATT
—
LONDON
1687 – 1701

THOMAS
WYATT
—
LONDON
1723

JOHN
WYNNE
—
LONDON
1746

JAMES
YATES
—
BIRMINGHAM
1800 – 1840
This mark used
also by
YATES & BIRCH
and also
YATES, BIRCH
& SPOONER,
Birmingham up to
1840 – 1850

LAWRENCE
YATES
—
LONDON
1740 – d. 1774

RICHARD
YATES
—
LONDON
1775 – 1794

EDWARD
YORKE
—
LONDON
1721 – d. 1747

A... H...
—
EDINBURGH
1660

B... G...
—
EDINBURGH
1630

C... C...
—
EDINBURGH
1675

C... T...
—
EDINBURGH
1675

H... R...
—
EDINBURGH
1663

M... L...
—
EDINBURGH
1600

Unidentified
Touchmarks

E. A. — LONDON c. 1670		W. A. — LONDON c. 1670	
E. A. — LONDON c. 1685		C. B. — LONDON c. 1678	
I. A. — LONDON c. 1670		I. B. — c. 1670–90	
N. A. — EDINBURGH 1733		P. B. — LONDON c. 1670	
E. G. & R. A. — c. 1710		R. B. — LONDON c. 1678	
S. A. — LONDON c. 1670		I. B. — LONDON c. 1680	
S. A. — LONDON c. 1670		T. B. — LONDON c. 1670	

A. T. B.
—
LONDON
c. 1690

I. C.
—
LONDON
c. 1670

T. B.
—
LONDON
c. 1688

I. C.
—
LONDON
c. 1670

W. B.
—
LONDON
c. 1690

I. C.
—
LONDON
c. 1670–75

W. B.
—
LONDON
c. 1670

M. C.
—
LONDON
c. 1676–80

G. C.
—
LONDON
c. 1676

T. C.
—
LONDON
c. 1670

F. C.
—
LONDON
c. 1670

H. D.
—
LONDON
c. 1680–85

I. C.
—
LONDON
c. 1670

R. D.
—
c. 1690

R. D.
—
c. 1716

B. E.
—
LONDON
c. 1670–75

W. E.
—
LONDON
c. 1670

I. F.
—
LONDON
c. 1800

I. G.
—
LONDON
c. 1692

T. G.
—
LONDON
c. 1675

W. G.
—
LONDON
c. 1670

D. C. H.
—
LONDON
c. 1670

E. H.
—
LONDON
c. 1663–1690

E. H.
—
LONDON
c. 1668

E. H.
—
LONDON
c. 1670

E. H.
—
LONDON
c. 1670

I. H.
—
LONDON
c. 1663–1670

I. H.
—
LONDON
c. 1663–80

I. H. — LONDON c. 1670		I. I. — LONDON c. 1670	
I. H. — LONDON c. 1670		R. I. — EDINBURGH 1600	
T. H. — LONDON c. 1670		R. I. — LONDON c. 1668	
W. H. — LONDON c. 1680		R. I. — LONDON c. 1650–75	
H. I. — LONDON c. 1688		I. L. — LONDON c. 1663–70	
I. I. — LONDON c. 1670		H. M. — LONDON c. 1695	
I. I. — LONDON c. 1670		I. M. — LONDON c. 1668	

R. M.
—
LONDON
c. 1670

P. P.
—
LONDON
1668

W. M.
—
LONDON
c. 1666

R. P.
—
LONDON
1671

W. M.
—
LONDON
c. 1670

V. Q.
—
EDINBURGH
1600

W. M.
—
LONDON
c. 1820

W. P.
—
LONDON
c. 1670

I. N.
—
LONDON
c. 1676–80

C. R.
—
LONDON
1668

F. P.
—
LONDON
c. 1670

I. R.
—
LONDON
1663

H. P.
—
LONDON
c. 1670

S. A.
—
EDINBURGH
1631

I. S. — LONDON 1685			T. V. — EDINBURGH 1631	
T. S. — LONDON c. 1670			A. W. — LONDON c. 1670	
T. S. — LONDON c. 1663–70			I. W. — LONDON c. 1690	
T. S. — LONDON c. 1663–70			S. W. — LONDON c. 1675	
C. T. — LONDON c. 1660–75			T. W. — LONDON c. 1670	
H. T. — LONDON c. 1680				
W. T. — EDINBURGH 1685				

Bibliography

Bibliography

Below is a list of the more useful books and magazine articles which cover the subject specifically; many more have been published, and will be found of considerable help to the student of antique pewterware, but the list is too long for inclusion in this volume.

Books

BELL, MALCOLM
   Old Pewter, Geo. Newnes, London 1905. (Revised edition) 1913.

COTTERELL, HOWARD H.
   Old Pewter, its Makers and Marks, Batsford, London 1929 (Reprinted 1963).

INGLEBY WOOD, L.
   Scottish Pewterware and Pewterers, Edinburgh 1907.

MASSE, H. J. L. J.
   Pewter Plate, 1st Edition, Bell, London 1904. 2nd Edition (revised) 1911.
   Chats on Old Pewter, T. Fisher Unwin, London 1911.
   The Pewter Collector, Jenkins, London 1921.

MICHAELIS, R. F.
   Chats on Old Pewter (the original edition by Massé, of 1911, completely revised and substantially rewritten by R. F. Michaelis), Benn, London 1949.
   Antique Pewter of the British Isles, Bell, London 1955.
   A Short History of the Worshipful Company of Pewterers of London (and a Catalogue of Pewterware in its Possession), compiled for, and published privately by, the Worshipful Company, 1968.
   British Pewter, Ward Lock, London 1969.

PEAL, C. A.
   British Pewter for Pleasure and Investment, John Gifford,
   London, December 1970.

PRICE, F. G. HILTON
   Old Base Metal Spoons, Batsford, London 1908.

ULLYETT, KENNETH
   Pewter Collecting for Amateurs, Fredk. Muller, London
   1967.

WELCH, CHARLES
   History of the Worshipful Company of Pewterers, Blades,
   East & Blades, London 1902.

Some of the more important Articles in Antiques Journals

BISSET, LT.-COL. J. S.
   The Edinburgh Touchplates, Antique Collector, September
   1939.

COTTERELL, H. H.
   Evolution of the Pewter Plate, Antique Collection, October
   1931.
   Tavern Pewter, Antique Collector, August 1931.
   Dating the Pewter Tankard, Connoisseur, April 1932.
   Early Pewter Baluster Measures (An explanation of their lid
   markings), Apollo, May 1933.

MICHAELIS, R. F.
   English Pewter Porringers (in four parts) Apollo, July,
   August, September, October 1949.
   Old Pewter Wine Measures (in two parts), Antique Collector,
   February and August 1953.
   Capacity Marks on Old Pewter Wine Measures, Antique
   Collector, August 1954.
   Royal Portraits and Pewter Porringers, Antiques (U.S.A.),
   January 1958.
   More About English Commemorative Porringers, Antiques
   (U.S.A.), July 1960.
   Decoration on English Pewterware (in four parts), Antique
   Collector, October 1963, February, August and December
   1964.

MINCHIN, CYRIL C.
A Berkshire Pewter Collection (2 parts), Apollo, April and July 1946.
Flagons and Tankards in Pewter, Antique Collector, February 1952.

PEAL, CHRISTOPHER A.
Tankards, and 'Housemarks' on Early Baluster Measures, Apollo, June 1949.
Notes on Pewter Baluster Measures, and Their Capacities, Apollo, January 1950.
Romano-British Plates and Dishes, Proc. Cambridge Antique Society, Vol. LX 1967.

PORT, CHARLES, G. J.
Some Uncommon Pieces of Pewter (in five parts), Connoisseur, April and December 1917, October 1918, September 1921 and March 1925.

SUTHERLAND GRAEME, A. V.
Pewter Church Plate, Connoisseur (Part I), October 1936; (Part II), Apollo 1940.
Pewter Spoons, Connoisseur, December 1947.
The Society of Pewter Collectors, Connoisseur, December 1933.

The London Touchplates are illustrated in photogravure (actual size) in:

Welch's *History of the Pewterers' Company* 1902.
Massé's *Pewter Plate*, 2nd edition 1911.
Cotterell's *Old Pewter* . . . 1929.